Marriage Maps and Driven Destinies

Marriage Maps and Driven Destinies

Mary Sexson

Lylanne Musselman

Chatter House Press
Indianapolis, Indiana

Marriage Maps and Driven Destinies

Copyright© 2023
by Mary Sexson & Lylanne Musselman

Cover Design by Penny Dunning

All rights reserved.

Except for brief quotations embodied in critical articles and reviews in newspapers, magazines, radio or television, no part of this book may be reproduced in any form or by any means electronic, mechanical, or by any information storage and retrieval system without written permission from the publisher.

For information:
Chatter House Press
7915 S Emerson Ave, Ste B303
Indianapolis, IN 46237
chatterhousepress.com

ISBN: 978-1-937793-53-1

Dedication by Mary Sexson

This book is dedicated
to my husband, Jack,
who lived an amazing life

and
Lylanne Musselman
my Poetry Sister

Dedication by Lylanne Musselman

To my daughters, Keli & Alison
&
To Mary, my Poetry Sister

Acknowledgments

Married: The Grammar of Love

"Where is Your Placenta Buried" - *Company of Women, New and Selected Poems* (Chatter House Press 2013)

"The Grammar of Love, Under the Porchlight" - *Last Stanza Poetry Journal* Issue #5 (Stack Freed Press 2021)

"Swallowing Grief" - *Last Stanza Poetry Journal* Issue #10 (Stack Freed Press 2022)

"In the Constellation of Cancer" - *Of Rust and Glass* (January 2023)

"Your Own Eclipse" - *The Flying Island Journal*, March 2023

"Wild Peacocks" - *The Flying Island Journal*, July, 2023

Driven: A Life Well-Traveled

I would like to thank the editors of these publications where my poems originally appeared:

"Church Street" – *Last Stanza Poetry Journal*

"Cruising, 1975" – *A Charm Bracelet for Cruising* & *It's Not Love, Unfortunately*

"Driven" – *Huron River Review* & *It's Not Love, Unfortunately*

"I Pass Over its Bridges" – *The Indianapolis Review*

"Love, Love, Love" – *The Ramingo's Porch* & *Company of Women New & Collected Poems*

"Running Late" – *Cincinnati Writers Project Anthology*

"Sunday Drive" – *Flying Island* & *It's Not Love, Unfortunately*

"Unlicensed Driver" – *Car Poems* & *It's Not Love, Unfortunately*

Table of Contents

Married: The Grammar of Love

    The Grammar of Love 3
    Morning Blue 4
    Psychic Damage: Reflection 5
    This Vantage Point 6
    Hot Date 7
    Where is Your Placenta Buried?............................8
    When the Bike Broke...9
    Under the Porch Light 10
    Married 11
    Progeny 12
    Early Morning ER Run...13
    Heart Attack...14
    Reflections on a Bum Ticker...............................15
    You'll Never Shovel Snow Again 16
    Wild Peacocks...17
    Your Own Eclipse 18
    Sifting Through Moon Shine................................19
    Reflections on a Marriage 20
    Newton's Law, Abided 21
    This Angst..22
    Swallowing Grief..24
    Friends in High Places 25
    Between Life and Death 26
    This is What We Do 27
    In the Constellation of Cancer.............................29

Driven: A Life Well-Traveled: New & Collected Poems

I Pass Over its Bridges 33
Lover of Lights and the Dark 34
Bittersweet 35
Dad's '59 Chevy 36
Sunday Drive 37
Unlicensed Driver 38
Driven 40
Cruising, 1975 41
Too Much Snow 42
Winter Slides Out of Favor 43
A Saturday in Toledo 44
Running Late 45
Driving Prey 46
How My Words Got Away 47
Coupling 48
Flashbacks 49
Love, Love, Love 50
The Red Fox 51
The Wild Turkey, 2020 52
Winter Protest 53
Before Seatbelts 54
A Merging Reflection 55
I Believed in Love 57
Church Street 58
Avian Observations 60
A Short History of Vacations 61

Married: The Grammar of Love

New and Selected Poems

by Mary Sexson

Mary Sexson

The Grammar of Love

I caught the second wind of my life
sometime in my forties,
when our love became more
than a common noun, and we found
a path back to each other's
way of thinking.
There were days of weeping,
certainly, that mixed
with the remnants of our spite,
and threatened us both
with the notion of losing
all over again.

But we rose up each day
through the murky waters of resolution,
restless for the touch of each other
and the sounds
of our soothing voices.

A resurrection of what was lost
laid before us.

And our love became the predicate,
stated in the nominative case:
Love is bitterness
Love is redemptive
Love is grace.

Morning Blue

Your mornings are colored blue,
filtered through a sieve of worry,

money, work, kids,
your unhealthy heart.

You can usually shake it off
by nine, wash it off with
shaving lather, brush it out
with the fine-toothed comb
you use to put each hair in place.
When you are ready to walk
out the door and take on
the day you can feel hopeful
for what may come.

There are times, though,
when the transformation
has not yet happened,
you are still saturated
in it, awash in the ink
of doubt and hopelessness.
The sun will not lift it,
it's too heavy a load
even for beauty to take on.
You must bear it
all that day, clutch it
in your hands like
an unclaimed suitcase
whose owner has already
boarded another plane.

Psychic Damage: Reflection

I do not always have the words
to tell you how I am feeling right
at that moment. I may stutter

and trip over syllables, or hold back
for want of better phrasing.

But when you talk about the fact
that you will embark on a project
with or without me I can feel

the thrum of noise in my head
that tells me I cannot withstand

the feelings that are there beneath it,
collating and stapling themselves
together in an optic bouquet

of reds and oranges. I can minimize
the psychic damage by changing

course, opting for a different road
to the same destination so how I
get there no longer matters, only that
I get there and you are waiting.

This Vantage Point

On the anniversary of your
sixty-first year, you are reveling
in your family, and save for the
prodigal son who has not yet
returned, we are all in attendance,
a luncheon and the requisite cake,
your grandson sharing his icing
with no complaints.

You can sit back now, from this
vantage point, and have a look
at what you've done, where we've been
as a family, walking this road together.
I hope you would say there's not a thing
you'd change, nothing to regret,
especially since you pulled off living
through two near-fatalities. I believe
you'd say it has been more than enough,
this life spread like a fine feast before you,
and I, your lucky companion, would have to agree.

Hot Date

You met me on the battery aisle
at the Harbor Freight store, and we
shopped for a good extension cord
with a surge protector. We moseyed
up to the wood splitters where you toyed
with the notion of buying one, a manual
version for only $119.00. Such a deal
and how quick it would make firewood
of the fallen ash tree in our neighbor's yard,
the wood ours if we could split and haul it.

I wanted gardening gloves, and new
pruning shears, and you fretted about
the pair that cost $12.99 but realized
they were on sale, so go ahead, and I did.
We looked at tarps, flashlights, hoses,
and scissors. Our 25% off coupon
could only be used on the most
expensive item but we walked to lunch
feeling like we'd gotten a heck of a deal.

Where is Your Placenta Buried?

If we were good keepers
of the Seri language we'd know
this is the most important question.
It will tell us where we are from,
and how far we have come.

I happen to know where yours
is buried, from the mystical story
of your birth, the picture
of your father and the doctor drinking
at the kitchen table while you labored
to be born in the room just above them.
Ingrained in my memory as if
it was my own, and now it is a myth
in our family, the story we told our kids
when they were younger so they
would have a real sense of you.

Your dad and the old doctor
drank themselves silly while
the Christian Science midwife
brought you into this world,
the last of five, and the only one
your mother birthed
as her faith directed.

They buried your placenta under
the sugar maple in the side yard, a tree
I can pass by on a good walk any day.
Comforting to know that we know
exactly where you are from.

When the Bike Broke

We journey well together, you and I,
witnessed by the ability to handle
unexpected events, heart attacks,
car accidents, kids doing drugs,
or financial woes.
                        We have
whooped and hollered at times,
but mostly we just figure it out
and go on. There is not much fanfare,
sometimes emotions and tears,
yet we always look to each other
when a crisis is at hand, knowing
the other will help get this thing solved
the best we can.
                       Today
far from home your bike broke while
we rode. No worries, we walked it
to our destination, saw the movie
we'd come to see, and then I rode home
to get the car and come back for you
and that broken bicycle. No hubbub,
no fretting.
                       You took a walk while
you waited, I grabbed a snack
at home before I came for you,
both of us happy about our day.

Under the Porch Light

If we let our minds drift back
to the beginning of our love
perhaps we can see how
it shaped us, how we were
sculpted by the bliss and the
fear of it, the opening up
of ourselves to it, how we both
lay down, at times, and let it
wash over us.
                    You kissed me
under a porch light many
years ago, such a quick
solemn moment, yet it
bound me to you. I can
show you the layers of such
movements, and how they
have kept me near you all
these years. It was never
the spectacular or the perfect,
rather the simplest of motions,
your lips to mine.

Married

We've learned how to sit
next to each other in a movie,
who gets which seat, which
arm rest, whether or not

we're in the back row, or down front
where the action is. I'm forever
worried the talkers will keep
talking even when the movie

starts, you are calm and collected,
and know it will be fine once
the lights are dim. I only whisper
to you when I need to know

what else that actor was in,
who did the music for this film,
and whether or not we
will share any popcorn tonight.

Married: The Grammar of Love

Progeny

What does it look like
from sixty-two, this long glance
back to where you've been.

I want to know every frame
in that long Kodachrome curl
of shot after shot of you, blonde

and Norse looking, that Viking nose
a dead give-away to your handsome
DNA strand, the one mingled now

in our own children's chromosomes.
And I wanted that, more than
anything you could have given me,

those delicate strands, lovely y's
and x's, twenty-three perfect pairs
matched up in the beauty of our offspring.

Early Morning ER Run

You, on a gurney,
reminiscent of
another time, yet
not so distant I
didn't recognize
the look of fear
you had in your eyes.

Norm the nurse fooled
us all with his
football shoulders
that pushed
against the seams
of his cute blue
scrubs. He

soft-shoed you,
made you think
everything was
going to be dandy
but the pressure
persisted and we
called out, together,
for one more look
at an EKG, and there
it was plain as day

easy to see now,
make note of
and cluck over,
till they send you
straight away
to the Cath Lab
for some repairs
under your hood.

Heart Attack

Now we can put a price
on your freedom, you wanting
to be back home on your own,
no one watching you,
no one drawing blood
every few hours.
You pace this room
in the silly gown
they gave you, your ass
hanging out the back, electrodes
on your chest that had
tethered you to a bed,
to machines that beeped as if
leaving a message in code.
The blood pressure cuff
still inflating and releasing,
registering all the numbers,
data to crunch later
between a computer's teeth.
Doctors barely look at you, just
the machines, the digital
numbers blinking, blaring
red and green. Now you move
to a chair, sit yourself
down and wonder
how you got here,
how will you get home?

Reflections on a Bum Ticker

How do we mend this heart
of yours, broken as it is,
fluttering in the wind
of your lungs and the mighty
gusts they blow. I cannot
soothe you, calm you,
schmooze you. I can
whisper in your ear,
say the things you want
to hear, but I cannot fix
that bum ticker of yours.
I can stretch across your
great divide, pull and push
you into a more together
place, if you will just, please,
not resist. I will be your byline,
your frontline, your backdrop,
catch your fall from grace,
and push you into the place
of lofty desires, a new view
from above, if you'll mend
your heart and deliver me your love.

Married: The Grammar of Love

You'll Never Shovel Snow Again

Cardiac recovery is a world in itself,
concerned phone calls, naps,
gentle walks down the block,
(no rowdy stuff, no two hour treks
for a while) a movie maybe,
an hour or two watching TV,
a bit of time with your grandson,
another nap before lunch.

And you read
the materials the doctors gave you,
unscramble the information
that's relevant, decode the tricky
medical lingo, and pay attention
to the list of what you may
and may not do. So
you'll never shovel snow again.
I think you can live with that,
the rest of it
we'll get to when we get to it,
because yes, your life goes on.

Wild Peacocks

Eight-thousand miles can take
a toll, even on an iPhone,
and so your voice echoes, fades
in and out as you tell me about
the wild peacocks, their call,
their strutty selves walking
the grounds where you
are staying.
         Our son guides you
each day through this maze
of newness. You, who clung
to home as if it were your lifeboat,
now wander on evening walks
with him in the dust and heat
of southern India, washing
 your clothes in a bucket
and scooping your food
with your hand.
         I wonder at
the sound of it, whether I
could navigate such a distance,
could listen to the peacock's call.

Your Own Eclipse

We waited for the eclipse's darkness
together, me running in and out
with our grandson to peer
through the homemade viewer
we'd fashioned from one
of his cereal boxes.

You stayed inside, still
tending to your heart, fresh
from an eclipse of its own,
some dark moon lumbering
through your bypass grafts,
shadowing the host, and bringing us
all down to our knees.

They say we won't see
a total eclipse for another seven years,
far enough away for me to wonder
if I'd view that one alone.
Or would you persevere, hold back
the tide that pushes closer to your shore,
even as we both ooh and aah
over the crescent shadows
dancing on our sidewalk.

Sifting Through Moon Shine

Sitting here sifting through the moon shine
that casts itself on the water, we are together

sharing bread and soup, recalling the day
as it survived itself, unraveling the fears

that catch us, like a hook in our sides.
We struggle to snap the line, get it to let go

but it snags itself on the romance of our emotions,
the fracture of our hearts as we bang against the truth

of walking through this moment barefoot
to get to the other side of beauty, newly cast in
watercolors

surrounded by an iron frame, unbreakable now,
like the fever of our love.

Married: The Grammar of Love

Reflections on a Marriage

I realize as I wipe the oily residue
from your late-night cooking

off the stove, close the cabinet
you left open, and put away the onion

left half-chopped on the counter,
that I can keep my mouth shut

so much more easily now, after
35 years, than I could a few

years back. I examine what this
might mean as I rinse off the cloth

and wipe again, putting a bit
of muscle into it this time.

Newton's Law, Abided

You seem to have been
the external force

that acted upon me, much
as Newton's first law

describes. I was in motion
and then you tugged gently

on my orbit, bringing me
into your own, where I

believe we learned,
very well, how to do
the motion together.

Swallowing Grief

I eat my way
through my grief. Cookies

will assuage my pain. Cake
will soften the blow

of no surgery possible. Dinner out
with friends allows me

to feel like a normal human being
for a few hours,

where no one is doing the math
to figure out how long you've got.

You've dropped your weight
by more than thirty pounds

through this ordeal and I
have loaded a few of them on,

absorbed from the detritus
of what you have sloughed off.

So we sit and lick these
dreamy drumstick cones, savor

their exquisite taste,
and the closeness
they have brought us.

Friends in High Places

When her father, so sick
from chemo and radiation,
inspires his daughter, who is in recovery,
to reach out to an old drug dealer
who can tell her what might
cut the nausea or make him want to eat.

The juxtaposition of these needs,
the starkness of who we know
in this life, the dealer, the doctor,
the healer, the friend who tells us
that a bit of THC oil under his tongue
can make a bowl of peaches
more palatable, that he may not
vomit when he's done,
that this funny little bit of nature
can actually help him to stomach it
even as his body winces against
the poisons he's already swallowed.

This Angst

When I drop down
the search window on Google
the name of your cancer
is there, waiting for me
to search again, peck up
the crumbs of information,
hop over to this other
medical site that will tell me
which stage is what and how
each one offers its own
chances of recovery,
if you're lucky.

This rare cancer that nobody
knew the name of
until yesterday just became
a household word to us
and it already has you
in the clutches of anxiety.
You sit with closed eyes
telling me you're meditating
but I know you're not.
I can see how your leg
is crossed and jiggling,
your hands clasped tightly
across your lap,

Mary Sexson

the earmarks of you
awash in bad thoughts
and little hope. Your daughter
wants to set you free
from this angst, get you
on a good antidepressant.
Your grandson offers only
the purity of his thoughts
for each day. And I,
well, I only know I cannot
bear the loss of you.

Married: The Grammar of Love

Between Life and Death

We have no dates to enter
into some serious journal
that will tell us when we're done,
when you're done, when
your body is done, when the over
is really over and not some
temporary reprieve, itself a rug
that can be pulled out easily
from under your grip on this life.

Relentless as the sun that fades
our curtains, as the nausea
that pushes up when you smell
my cooking, as the knowledge
that this is not yet over.

The crush of morning
lays across my shoulders
a metaphor for your sickness
that we must face again today.

Mary Sexson

This is What We Do

I throw the used Kleenex down
seemingly into
the wastebasket that
has been in that spot
for the last twenty-five years
but has now been moved,
like everything else
in your life, our lives,
pushed to a different place
to make room for this new normal
we are loathe to embrace.

We've jerry-rigged
the bathroom with
a bedside commode
that straddles our toilet
so you can maneuver
yourself on and off.
We put a bed
in the dining room,
a walker
beside it, another walker
in the front hallway
and there's one
in the trunk of the car,
just in case.

Married: The Grammar of Love

> We have a lot of
> just-in-cases:
> remote light switches
> coded pill bins
> bolstered chairs
> that you can get up and out of,
> cups of water set everywhere
> so that you will ideally
> drink water all day long, this
> an edict from your Physical Therapist
> who comes twice a week
> to help you learn how to live, again.

Mary Sexson

In the Constellation of Cancer

I am floating untethered
through the scope
of your illness, an old star
rising on the edge
of your galaxy, passing
its nebulas and dwarf stars,
past constellations
we knew the names of
when we were young.

Now I am an astronaut
and you a diminished star system
on the brink of losing your light.
But I am fastened
to your burning core
and we still hover within
our own Milky Way,
the one we have mapped
and know our way through,
here in the second quadrant
of the Northern Hemisphere.

I need this familiar place, if I
am to guide you through it
while you close your eyes
against the pain, against the futility
that seems to underscore it.
If we are to cross
this island universe that has held us
throughout our time I have to know
which way is up.

Mary Sexson is author of the newly released *Her Addiction An Empty Place at the Table* (Finishing Line Press). Her other books include the award-winning *103 in the Light, Selected Poems 1996-2000* (Restoration Press), and *Company of Women, New and Selected Poems* (Chatter House Press). She co-authored the upcoming book, *Marriage Maps and Driven Destinies*, to be published by Chatter House Press in the Fall of 2023. Sexson's poetry has appeared in many publications. Her work is part of the Inverse Poetry Archives for Hoosier Poets. One of her poems is in the Polaris Trilogy, heading for the moon in 2024. Find her at masexson.wordpress.com, and at Poetry Sisters on FaceBook.

Driven: A Life Well-Traveled

New and Collected Poems

by Lylanne Musselman

Driven: A Life Well-Traveled

Lylanne Musselman

I Pass Over its Bridges

I cross the Mississinewa River
to get groceries, to meet friends,
to go to church, to carry art to exhibits,
to visit the cemetery where my ancestors are buried.

Each time I pass over its bridges: singing
"Can't Buy Me Love" at the top of my lungs
while riding in the backseat of Mom and Bobo's Buick
on our trips for ice cream at Dairy Dream, memories
of Mom before dementia set in, always driving,

of Dad laughing when we'd cross
the wooden bridge in Granville,
its rickety racket making me panic,
of my own daughters giggling over boys
in the backseat as we drove home
from miniature golf or from Pizza King,

of Mark singing "Sun Arise" along with Alice Cooper
in his red Vega after one of our movie dates,
of riding school bus number 26 to Delta on Highway 3,

Bill and I sailing south, heading toward our honeymoon
in Florida, of crossing it pregnant, traveling home
with two daughters three years apart,

of driving to work in Muncie
selling sweepers as a single mom,
after carrying years of marital
fear, unkind words, and tears
across that bridge, of seeing
that bald eagle perched
among autumn leaves,

after leaving mom in hospice,
driving home, alone,
across the familiar river.

Lover of Lights and the Dark

Mom said when I was a baby and
she couldn't get me to calm down,
she and dad would take me for car rides
at night. She distracted me from fussing
by saying, "Look at the pretty lights!"

Night has always been my time.
Millions of stars lighting up the sky,
night is when my energy strikes.
It's when my creativity flows onto the page.
After midnight's stroke, I write, paint, and read.

I'm not one that fears the dark,
with others it causes worry and dread:
Conjuring up deep secrets, scary thoughts –
thinking of the dead. For me, the dark
brings comfort, lifts my spirits.
I always notice lights – city lights,
rural lights, colorful and luminous,
against a dark backdrop –
they please me into peace.

Bittersweet

You remember
riding in the backseat,
of that '66 Bonneville,
Mom telling Dad
to pull over, she's
spotted some
bittersweet twining
around a wiry fence
on that drab rural road.
You watch as she
puts on gloves and
runs over to cut some
blooming vines with
those funky looking
scissors, never understanding
why she always was on
the lookout for those
treasured orange pods,
growing along the countryside,
Dad always a willing accomplice.
Decades later, curious about those
fiery bright berries, you Google them
to find they're aggressive, and
considered noxious weeds.
Mom and Dad no longer
around to ask the motive, now
you've grown bittersweet.

Dad's '59 Chevy

I liked how the back of the car resembled cat's eyes to a three-year-old who got to ride in the big backseat. Back then, men always drove. There were no seatbelts – so I stood on the "hump" and looked over the front seat between Dad and Mom, watching for oncoming cars, cows and pigs in barnyards, through the windshield. I laughed at Dad making "moo" and "oink" sounds whenever we'd pass them by. I remember his cherry pipe tobacco haze hanging in our air. I loved our after-supper rides in that car across back roads between Eaton and Albany for a swirling soft serve ice cream at Dairy Dream. I never got to order the chocolate dip cone, too messy when chunks of chocolate would drop on my clothes. Still, Mom made me sit with a newspaper over my lap, so no soft melting drips would fall onto Dad's immaculate light blue cloth seats. A few years later, Dad traded that car in when he was ready for a newer one. I cried at the loss of that car since no other looked like our Impala with tail fins, fender and taillights that called to mind a cat face.

Sunday Drive

In the backseat of our '66 green Pontiac Bonneville, my view was of the back of my parent's heads: dad with dark wavy hair, hands on the steering wheel, his pipe smoke swirling upward and back into my space; mom with coiffed hair, in the passenger's seat chewing her Juicy Fruit gum. I was along for the ride each Sunday going to see my grandma who lived an hour away in Kokomo. I loaded up the backseat with my favorite stuffed animals and a few books in hopes of making time cruise a bit faster. I hated leaving other beloved belongings behind, feeling guilty for all that couldn't go. I loved listening to the radio, Fort Wayne's strong AM station, WOWO. The Beatles, Neil Diamond, The Supremes, Tammy Wynette and George Jones were played one after the other. I could've done without country, but dad preferred it to my favorites. I sang along with all songs that came on, even D-I-V-O-R-C-E. Mom marveled how I knew every word, saying she wished I memorized my homework like I did those songs. I worried all new song lyrics would be used up by the time I became a mom, driving with my own kids riding in the backseat.

Unlicensed Driver

My first memory of driving
was around 15 –
I was waitressing
at my uncle's restaurant.

Mom, dad, my aunt and
uncle had gone home
early for an adult party
later that evening.

My two younger cousins
assigned to stay with me,
were to be brought
home by our designated driver –

Bill, a policeman
already drinking,
was ready
for that party in Eaton;

he continued to drink
but didn't want to drive,
so he told me I had to.
I was excited to drive

Lylanne Musselman

8 miles on real [rural] roads
but scared of him –
hovering [always] at 6'6" and
unusually gruff. This night

he resembled a jolly giant,
as he instructed me to "get
behind the wheel" of his [rusty]
red Jeep, laughing at how mad

my parents would be. Livid
they were; yet, we all made it
home safe; me yearning
to drive again and again.

Driven

At 16, I test drove a '57 Chevy, the car
that flares in the back – like wings.
It was turquoise and white and didn't
have power steering. It was hard
for my young arms to turn.

So my first car was a 1964 Buick
Skylark Convertible, white exterior and
red vinyl seats and dashboard.
My parents bought the car
from twenty-three-year-old Terry –
a licentious grease monkey
who took me for a test drive
in the country and a spin
I wouldn't forget.

That car and Terry
shifted my life –
one would leave me
stranded on train tracks or in the middle
of busy intersections, one would leave me
directionless on a well-traveled road,
empty, fueled with doubts.

Lylanne Musselman

Cruising, 1975

We drove the small town strip in Bill's Corvette,
from the carwash on the north side and around

the A & W Root Beer stand, next to the cornfield,
back and forth on State Road 3, going nowhere.

I sang "Love Will Keep Us Together," out loud,
even though I knew it wasn't love. I felt safe

with Bill who wasn't like the small town policeman
who violated my virginity when I was fifteen.

In the rearview mirror – reflections of a female friend,
in her small Vega with a bronze body, made my heart skip.

Oblivious of the implications, Bill and I revved our drive-by
love – eight years and two daughters away from a divorce,

racing towards a lifetime linked by grandchildren and silent
stares, two strangers who tried to drive their dreams home.

Too Much Snow

The older I get, the more I dislike snow.
Yet, living through the Blizzard of '78
is a favorite memory. I was skeptical
when I saw *Blizzard Warning* pop up
in the bottom corner of the TV screen.
Blizzards don't happen in Indiana.

A new mom with a 9-month-old baby,
my husband was uncharacteristically
working out of town, and I worried
he wouldn't make it back. As the snow
started piling up that night, he did.
There was comfort in our little family
being together in our small home.

Snow kept falling at a pace
we'd never seen. A day later
I was shocked into stopping neighbor boys
from walking on top of my husband's
prized '69 Corvette convertible, covered
by a major snow drift.

When the snow finally stopped,
snow drifts reached rooftops
of houses. It was weeks before
we were able to travel on highways.
When we did, it was through snow
tunnels, orange flags tied
to car antennas so others knew
another car was coming through.

Lylanne Musselman

Winter Slides Out of Favor

I used to embrace the snow
with angel wings, the deeper
the snow drifts the better.

I loved the heavy snow of December.
Glittering intensified white
showers in street lights

highlighted Santa's sleigh
and all eleven reindeer
landing on our roof.

Even when it had no chimney,
I never worried that Santa would pass
over my house as long as there was snow.

But snowy dreams turned
into icy nightmares – after a basketball game,
when our car slid into a ditch and through a barbed wire fence.

Unscathed, but scared my friends and I walked miles for help
to dig our car out from the snow and ice
that chipped away winter's wonder.

A Saturday in Toledo

Driving through the streets of Toledo
Glenn argues with the lady
who voices her directions
from his Magellan GPS.
She insists over and over
that he turn right
onto interstate 475,
but instead he continues east
showing me the original Tony Packo's
and the waterfront, where plans
for commercial development
along the Maumee just might
strengthen the rusty health
of this crippled city.

We arrive at our destination:
Maumee Bay State Park,
and walk the winding Mouse Trail
where black wooly worms inch predictions
of a long harsh winter
in front of us
crickets leap in the sun,
Midwestern-fat gulls dip and fly
in search of fast food
littered along the desolate beach,
and cry for attention
as we navigate
back to the wide open asphalt.

Lylanne Musselman

Running Late

Mama Cass warned me, "Monday Monday,
can't trust that day." My morning clock ticks
Monday minutes off. Sun rises, blinds me
through my front windshield –
radio on – getting Sirius with The Morning
Jolt. Speedometer reads 69, floor pedal down,
too late to slow down, cop car heads westbound –.
in my rearview mirror his brake lights shine. U-turn
into my eastbound lane. I'm traveling 55 now
but he passes several cars and pulls behind me.
Red and blue lights flash dance on top of his car.
I pull into the vacant Fremont Tractor Supply lot.
As I sit waiting for my fine, other cars squeal by.
Monday consequences calculate in my mind –
late to class, more money gone, calls to the office,
lost time, more money gone, lost luck,
morning sucks even more on Monday.

Driving Prey

Driving the highway
during the day, I see
hawks on the lookout,
as snow blinds landscape
claustrophobic as fog.
Must make having hawk eyes
a treasure, unless you're a
small morsel at the disposal
of a hungry predator
with sharp talons.

Sometimes driving in the snow
at night, it seems like semis
are predators, moving in on
smaller morsels, tossing
their weight around for the kill –
that might not make much sense
to anyone not on the road
white-knuckled, and praying
they're not the prey
this time.

Lylanne Musselman

How My Words Got Away

Dusty drives us north to Ann Arbor,
Betsy riding shotgun, loud
laughter and idle chatter,
finally summer break,
Glenn and I in the backseat,
a tiny spider dangles between us.

The spider shimmies down
its web, crawls onto my journal
lying between us. Sensing the urgency
to rid the culprit before Dusty freaks and
crashs us crumpled into a ditch,
he picks up my journal to flick
away the unwanted passenger.

The back window lowers slow,
tiny spider dances square across the cover,
Swoosh. Out the open window spider and journal,
filled with free writing in search of new poems, flies.
Splat! A semi crushes the spine of my lines, left for dead
in the fast lane of US 23, south of Dundee. Everything silent.
Followed by nervous laughter. A friendship put to a road test
over the loss of words between us.

Coupling

Driving from
Indianapolis to Toledo
after a wedding – the motion
of two people in love coming
together for life. I wonder
if such an emotion will
ever catch up with me –
to find another to go
along on my journey
moving forward like that
flock of geese flying south
in unison, or the train cars
hitched together
gliding effortlessly on
a long ride.

Lylanne Musselman

Flashbacks

On the highway, near Daleville,
a place I resided while married
to one of my husbands, I notice
a silver Cavalier in the lane beside me
at the stoplight, a woman driving,
a man in the passenger seat,
his arms and mouth flailing.

When the light changes, I accelerate
away from this unsettling scenario.
I check my rearview mirror.
I see the man continue his antics.
It makes me nervous – fearful
he's going to make this woman crash –
reminds me of an ex-husband
who picked fights with me
in the car while I was driving.

Sometimes when he drove
he would abruptly pull off
the side of the road, and
I could feel the semi's pull of death
as they'd pass by and the car
would shiver and shake like I did.
But the time that really rushes back
is when he told me to pull over and
I refused until I reached a stop sign,
so he jumped out of the vehicle
and rolled into the ditch.
I look back at this couple,
my heart pounds hard
as I see their passenger door open
as we're all driving...me over the speed limit
because I don't want to be part of this
mad man's carnage.

I look back and the silver car is gone.
It's as if it vaporized into thin air.

Love, Love, Love

I laugh at the idea of love.
I hear Delilah on the radio schmoozing
with callers on her all night love fest
as I drive, from Indianapolis back home
to Toledo, passing the hours by listening to sappy
tales of romance – what a joke,
as I relive past loves with each love song
she spins into the air so sweetly.
I don't love the idea of love anymore –
this once hopeless romantic
truly has had enough of the "Silly Love Songs,"
like the ones that McCartney and Lennon sold
in catchy tunes for impressionable youths
to believe in the perfect love, the happy ever after,
the match made in heaven, the kind of romance that
      never ends,
"Love Me Do," "From Me to You," "Love, love, love...,"
      and after all
the failed attempts at romance and wedded bliss,
I certainly don't "long for yesterday," or a late night
chat with the love seductress, Delilah.

Lylanne Musselman

The Red Fox

You were ready
to cross the road
in front of me,
as I slowed my car
to cross the railroad
you stopped
in your tracks.
Your dark eyes
met mine. You looked
scared. I marveled at
your red coat
that matched
the autumn leaves
making a beautiful
backdrop behind you.
Your black feet, and
pointy ears, that fluffy
tail a sharp contrast –
a perfect picture
but with a pickup truck
on my tail, I can't
take time to snap
your photo. You turn,
run away into bushes,
I wonder what tale
you carry back
to your pack.

The Wild Turkey, 2020

You stood in the middle of the road
enjoying your independence in total
trust I would yield to your presence.

A fellow female on a journey this
damp morn. Neither of us allowing
this rainy Monday to get us down.

We rejoice in the journeys of a new day,
a new autumn season, a new week,
I breathe a thanksgiving for us

both being here in this moment. Maybe
this was your first time to step out, or
maybe you've always been free to roam.

Your saturated feathers, striped and bold.
Your long legs carry a stunning body. I worry
as oncoming car lights shine at us in drizzle

on this desolate road. As I head west, I know
we're both staring into a looming winter horizon.
Will you be safe, will you wander away to live

another day? I see you in my rearview mirror.
I wish you another day of strolling fields and
forests, strong and tall.

On my way home, I think of you, and wonder
if you made it to your destination, I change route,
not wanting to witness if you didn't.

Lylanne Musselman

Winter Protest

I am over winter,
the sub-zero temperatures
and windchills that blow
lower and lower.

I didn't sign up
to be part of record-
breaking winters, or
to test how white
my knuckles can grip-
grasping the steering wheel
on black ice, while being
passed on the highway by big rigs
as if it's dry pavement and
I'm some little old lady
who shouldn't be on the road.

Who wants to hear
of students with frostbite,
of friends and colleagues
who've shattered ankles
while walking their dogs?

When hell freezes over?
With these winters
we're already there.

Before Seatbelts

I loved summers when I was ten years old, riding in Uncle Ben's '67 Corvette, along with my cousins, Little Ben and Gina. The car only sat two, but he would allow us to crawl in behind the seats and lie down. I was tall then and I hardly fit lengthwise, the nice thing was I was skinny, so I could squeeze in last. Uncle Ben would drive us up the country road from Eaton to Hartford City to his restaurant. I have no idea why none of us were allowed to sit in the passenger seat. Maybe Aunt Carolyn was with us, but I doubt it because she'd never let him drive 80 miles an hour, or 90, with kids in the car. But we liked it. We'd laugh and yell, "faster, faster!!" We loved it when we felt that surge. Now that I'm way older than he was at the time, and have daughters, grandchildren, and even great-grandchildren, what he was thinking? *What was I thinking?* I know when we're younger we all have a need for speed, as we think we are invincible, but those rides seem risky to me now. No wonder grandma, his mom, had a fit when we told her. He'd just laugh when he did it again.

Lylanne Musselman

A Merging Reflection

I see her reflection
in the purple AMC Gremlin,
a make and model
not around anymore.
But she is –
        just not her youthful image:
baby face, long wavy hair
reaching below her waist,
a tight young body with legs
going all the way up.

She thought she was loved
back then, by that man
who drove the Gremlin,
in her favorite color.
How her heart flipped
when she saw him coming
down the road. A visit making good
on that 2 AM sex talk
when he'd call from desk duty
in his police uniform.

She was so innocent back then,
so trusting. She believed
dreams would come true.
Now, I feel for that fifteen-year-old.
How I wish I could have
told her what her own mother
wouldn't:

*Stay away from that man.
He doesn't have your heart
in his. His interest being
able to brag to other men
how many young women
he wilted
at his wink and call.*

I embrace that young me
and remind her: *You survived,*
and her once tarnished image
fades into my rearview mirror.

Lylanne Musselman

I Believed in Love
after Carly Simon's *Coming Around Again*

I miss the romantic me,
the one who hopelessly believed
in love, so certain that when
someone broke my heart,
that a true love would be
coming around again.

After all, Carly sang:
there's more room in a broken heart,
and my heart is a mansion,
fooled into cruel expansion, when
I used to be willing to play the game.

I used to belt out these lyrics loud
in my car, on my way to be
with my lover, someone who
drove me crazy in the good ways.
We were so hopelessly romantic.

I know nothing stays the same.
I'm living proof. I have fallen apart.
It's no fun putting torn pieces back
together. I used to be in love.
I've forgotten to wish it to come
around for me again.

Church Street

The street I live on now
is the same street where I grew
into the sensitive, creative
I am now. A quiet small town
street where stray cats and squirrels
are more frequent travelers than cars,
this street paved my way to escape
an unexciting place, looking for
adventures when I was eighteen –

never dreaming at sixty
I would be summoned back
making this street my home
one more time. Moving my life
from Washington Street in Indy,
where a squirrel or cat never dare cross,
let alone walk the middle of that road.
A street where the whirring of traffic
and emergency sirens became background
noise to my busy city life. Not now –

on Church Street I can count cars
on one hand, passing by daily. The sirens
replaced by freight trains rumbling about
a mile away. Geese fly overhead, heading
to the Mississinewa (river, not the tavern),
just three blocks south. The street vacant
of huge Elm trees that lined my childhood
as I rode my bike back and forth to grandma's
house - one block west. Now, her familiar
house is for sale again.

Lylanne Musselman

Out the picture window: Chirp, chirp, chirp,
breaks the silence, the Northern Cardinal pair
arrive again, I've come to recognize them. In the air
more birdsong, sparrows and chickadees at the feeders.
I worry for the stray cats, I feed on my front porch too.
Sissy and Tilly, are pregnant again. I wonder
how many more mouths on this street I can feed.

Avian Observations

It never fails
while on my daily travels
I see a red-tailed hawk
on a fence post or in a tree,
watching for its next treat,
that time a bald eagle
flew across the bridge
along the river
right in front of me.
I often see a kestrel or two,
sometimes a rough-legged,
a red-shouldered, or a cooper's hawk.
When I drive from Eaton to Toledo,
to visit friends or go to the art museum,
I make a tally of how many hawks
I see along the way. Sometimes
they're out in plain view, in flight
or high on a pole, other times they blend
in among the tree limbs. The last trip
I counted twenty-six.
Then there's the smaller birds on wires,
one day at a stoplight I saw them playing
what appeared to be avian musical chairs,
they kept pushing each other over,
until the end one flew off, it came back
to the other end, and they all started pushing
each other over again.

Lylanne Musselman

A Short History of Vacations

I.
As a child, we never went on vacations.
Maybe Dad didn't want to take time off.
Maybe Mom wanted that money he made.
I didn't know I was missing out on trips
until others would talk at school about
California, Disneyland, or swimming
in the ocean. The only thing I could relate
was a Sunday drive to the Ohio River or
to see covered bridges here in Indiana.
We'd get lunch at Burger Chef
or Dairy Dream as a treat.

II.
In high school, I had the opportunity to go
to Toronto, Canada, with my art club.
We'd fly out of Indianapolis.
Mom said she wouldn't pay for it.
Not taking no for an answer, I paid
for the trip with money I made
from waitressing at Uncle Ben's restaurant.
I'm glad I went. I'll never forget my first
commercial plane ride with friends, our picture
with Morey Amsterdam, who was on our flight.
I loved Toronto, the clean streets, the architecture,
and the art museums, my first tequila sunrise and a thirst
for more travel and dreams of being an artist.

III
A few years ago, I went to Florida,
with my daughters and my grandchildren.
We drove down in one day in two cars,
we stayed in one huge condo in Orlando.
It was my first-time visiting Disney World,
although I'd made it to its gates on my ill-fated
honeymoon with their father over forty years ago.
We'd both decided not to go in as we'd taken ill –
with sunburns and fever. This time, my family enjoyed
Epcot, shopped souvenirs, and indulged in a lot of
     sweetness.
I needed this trip, a year after Dad died, a week respite
from caregiving Mom, who with dementia now,
will never know the smell or the feel of the ocean.

Lylanne Musselman is an award-winning poet, playwright, and visual artist. Her work has appeared in *Pank, Last Stanza Poetry Journal, Tipton Poetry Journal, The Indianapolis Review,* and *The Ekphrastic Review,* among many others, in addition to many anthologies. She is author of six chapbooks, and her seventh, *Staring Dementia in the Face* was published in 2023 by Finishing Line Press. Musselman is co-author of *Company of Women: New and Selected Poems* (Chatter House Press, 2013), and the author of the full-length poetry collection, *It's Not Love, Unfortunately* (Chatter House Press, 2018). A four-time Pushcart Prize nominee, her poems are included in the Inverse Poetry Archive, a collection of Hoosier poets, housed at the Indiana State Library.

www.ingramcontent.com/pod-product-compliance
Lightning Source LLC
Chambersburg PA
CBHW030137100526
44592CB00011B/922